The Blessings of a Surrendered Life:

Broken and Blessed

The Blessings of a Surrendered Life:

Broken and Blessed

E. C. Nakeli

© 2017 by E.C. Nakeli

Published by King's Word Publication

For your questions and publishing needs, write to: CMFI

40 S Church St

Westminster, MD 21157

E-mail: *ecnakeli@yahoo.com*

Printed in the United States of America

All rights reserved. No part of this publication may be reproduced, stored in retrieval systems, or transmitted in any form or by any means— for example, electronic, photocopy, recording— without the prior written permission of the publisher. The only exception is brief quotations in printed reviews.

To contact the author, write to:

E.C. Nakeli

40 S Church St Westminster, MD 21157

E-mail: *ecnakeli@yahoo.com*

The Blessing of a Surrendered Life/ E.C. Nakeli ISBN: 978-1-945055-04-1

Unless otherwise indicated, Scriptures references are from

THE HOLY BIBLE, NEW INTERNATIONAL VERSION®, NIV®

Copyright © 1973, 1978, 1984, 2011 by Biblica, Inc™

Used by permission. All rights reserved worlwide.

Table of Contents

Introduction 7
Part one: 10
The requirements of a surrendered life 10
Chapter 1 13
Devotion 13
   Passionate heart 14
      Seeking God 14
      Hunger and thirst after God 14
   Purged heart 15
   A heart poured-out to God 18
Chapter 2 21
Dependence 21
   Not leaning on your understanding 23
   Acknowledging the Lord in all your ways 24
   Do not be wise in your own eyes 27
Reckless abandon 27
   Our supreme example 29
Chapter 3 31
Decided Sanctification 31
   As we walk in the light 32
   The role of our wills 33
   A passion to be searched 35
Chapter 4 37
Determined Consecration 37
   The tent of your body 37

Guarding your tent	38
Purifying the Temple	39
The tent of your habitation	41
Chapter 5	43
Dead to Gain	43
The rich young ruler	43
Part two:	46
The battles and struggles of surrender	46
Chapter 6	48
Fear	48
Fear of the future	49
Fear of the unknown and the unfamiliar	49
Fear of man and systems	50
Fear of failure	52
See what it did to them	52
Chapter 7	55
Self-initiative	55
Learning from history	57
Chapter 8	59
Self-will	59
Peter's Arrogance	59
How it got Paul in trouble	60
Part 3:	63
The Rewards or Blessings of a Surrendered Life	63
Chapter 9	65
Confidence	65

A lesson from David 65

Chapter 10 68

Stability 68

Why do you need to stand firm? 69

Chapter 11 71

Boldness 71

   Let it take possession of you 72

Chapter 12 73

Emotional and Psychological Healing 73

   It is the gateway to fruitfulness 75

Chapter 13 77

Brightness of Life 77

It takes the Spirit and the word 78

The beauty of the morning 79

Chapter 14 82

Security 82

It's such a fortress 83

David lived in such a place 84

Chapter 15 86

Rest 86

The promise 86

The invitation 87

The path to rest 88

When you have entered rest 89

Chapter 16 91

People will seek your favor 91

Friends in High Places 92

Chapter 17 94

Riches in God 94

Chapter 18 97

Delight in the Almighty 97

The gateway to fulfillment 98

What it means 99

Chapter 19 102

Guaranteed Answer to Prayer 102

Chapter 20 105

Heaven's backing on your Decisions 105

Power to decree 106

Let this blow your mind 107

Chapter 21 108

Fulfilling your priestly role of intercession 108

Chapter 22 110

Fruitfulness 110

Because He says so 111

Conclusion 113

Introduction

In the world, the word surrender has a connotation of weakness, defeat, failure, or even loss. Since we all came from the world into the kingdom, our mindset has been programmed in the same way; those who surrender are weak, unable to defend themselves, stand up for their rights, or force their way through. In a sense, this is true. However, because the values of the kingdom to which we now belong are different from those of the world, surrender can take up a whole new meaning and value.

In the kingdom, God by His Spirit works in a lasting way only through surrendered men and women. When there is an important commission in the heart of the Almighty, He uses people who are weak, broken, and have completely surrendered to His Lordship, and through them demonstrates His unlimited power and grace. True and lasting blessings are the result of a surrendered life.

In this study, we will start by looking at the requirements of a surrendered life – what it takes to surrender to the Holy Spirit. Next we will look at the battles and struggles of surrender – internal and external conflicts faced in the process of surrendering, and finally we will look at the blessings of a surrendered life – the rewards that come when we have totally surrendered and yielded to Him.

My prayer for you is that as you go through this book, the blessed Holy Spirit will so work in you that you will begin the process of surrendering, if you are not there yet; take you through the struggles of surrendering, and bring you into the blessings of a surrendered life. I want to caution you that it can never be an accelerated process. He will take all His time, and put in place all His resources to work in you absolute surrender. The truth is that you will not be too far into it before you start realizing some of the blessings of surrendering. Though you cannot hasten the process, you can actually slow it down by not yielding to the workings of the Holy Spirit in you and through you.

> When there is an important commission in the heart of the Almighty, He uses people who are weak, broken, and have completely surrendered to His Lordship, and through them demonstrates His unlimited power and grace

This message on the blessings of a surrendered life was given me several years ago. Each time I wanted to write, something surfaced that revealed an unsurrendered area in my life. It has been a long and painful process of allowing the Lord to bring me to the place of absolute surrender. I may not have arrived yet but I have tasted of the fruits of what

I call "*Surrenderland*." Now my one desire is to come to that place of total and absolute surrender.

I invite you to come along as we explore the blessings of a surrendered life, taste of the fruits and make it your goal to experience total surrender to the Holy Spirit of endless grace and love. The journey to Surrenderland is a journey worth taking. All that is required is trust, commitment, and perseverance. But the benefits of arriving and making that land your habitation cannot be described in words. As we begin this journey I want you to pack everything you have, say goodbye to the land of self-struggles and take the determinant strides towards absolute surrender in Surrenderland.

Part one:

The requirements of a surrendered life

In this part of the book we are going to look at the qualifications or requisites for surrender. It should be noted that even these are the work of the Holy Spirit in us and through us; it takes a devoted person to produce total and absolute surrender. We will base our teaching here on two passages from the book of Job:

> "Yet if you devote your heart to him and stretch out your hands to him, if you put away the sin that is in your hand and allow no evil to dwell in your tent, then, free of fault, you will lift up your face; you will stand firm and without fear. You will surely forget your trouble, recalling it only as waters gone by. Life will be brighter than noonday, and darkness will become like morning. You will be secure, because there is hope; you will look about you and take your rest in safety. You will lie down, with no one to make you afraid, and many will court your favor." (Job 11:13-19)

> "Submit to God and be at peace with him; in this way prosperity will come to you. Accept instruction from his mouth and lay up his words in your heart. If you return to the Almighty, you will be restored: If you remove wickedness far from your tent and assign your nuggets to the dust, your gold of Ophir to the rocks in the ravines, then the Almighty will be your gold, the choicest silver for you. Surely then you will find delight in the Almighty and will lift up your face to God. You will pray to him, and he

will hear you, and you will fulfill your vows. What you decide on will be done, and light will shine on your ways. When people are brought low and you say, 'Lift them up!' then he will save the downcast. He will deliver even one who is not innocent, who will be delivered through the cleanness of your hands" (Job 22:21-30).

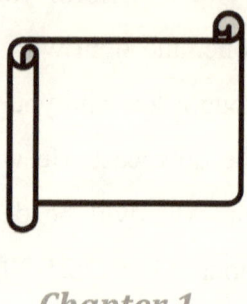

Chapter 1

Devotion

"Yet if you devote your heart to him..."

The first requisite of a surrendered life is a complete and total heart devotion to the Lord. The Holy Spirit seeks to work in us and bring us to a point where all of our heart is totally devoted to Him. This first requisite is very determinant to our walk with the Lord because all else we do in the Christian life is either accepted or rejected by the Lord based on the condition of our hearts.

A devoted heart is one that is conditioned and determined to go the whole way with the Lord. It is one that has refused to rationalize or compromise the commands of the Lord to suit the fallen standards of our time. A devoted heart is one that is passionate about nothing else but the Lord and those things the Lord may direct the heart to. The question is how does one bring his or her heart to the point of being devoted to the Lord?

Passionate heart

A heart that is devoted to the Lord is a heart that is filled with passion for God. David's heart was filled with passion for the Lord. If your heart is to be qualified as devoted to the Lord it must burn with passion for Him.

David said, "You, God, are my God, earnestly I seek you; I thirst for you, my whole being longs for you, in a dry and parched land where there is no water" (Ps 63:1) and "As the deer pants for streams of water, so my soul pants for you, my God. My soul thirsts for God, for the living God. When can I go and meet with God" (Ps 42:1-2)?

Both verses above demonstrate passion for God as described in the following characteristics:

Seeking God

"earnestly I seek you". A heart with passion for God is a heart that seeks to be in the presence of God; seeks an encounter with the God of the universe. Such a heart has come to the point of understanding that one encounter with the Lord has the potential to bring a lifetime transformation. Are you a seeker of God? Does your heart yearn for an encounter with the God of holiness and truth?

Hunger and thirst after God

"I thirst for you, my whole being longs for you". A heart on passion is a heart that hungers and thirsts for God; one which nothing else satisfies until it has met with God. To such a heart, the presence of God is food and drink and it satisfies both spirit and soul. The Lord wants us to run after

Him with a passionate desire to get hold of Him. The truth is that this desire can never arise from within us but must be placed there by God Himself, and He seeks to place the desire, hunger, and thirst for Him in each one of us.

> *A devoted heart is one that is conditioned and determined to go the whole way with the Lord. It is one that has refused to rationalize or compromise the commands of the Lord to suit the fallen standards of our time.*

When we set our hearts to pursue Him, He gets hold of us and brings us to the place where nothing else matters in this world. Sometimes you realize you get frustrated with everything and the company of no human being is able to satisfy you. Occupying yourself with things only leads to further dissatisfaction until you come face to face with the Lord and He begins to minister to you. Sometimes all you can do is just love the Lord and enjoy His awesome presence. This dissatisfaction with all else is evidence of a hunger and a thirst for God which is placed in our hearts by the Holy Spirit. If you lack passion in your heart for God and the things of God you can ask Him to sow in you a deep and insatiable hunger and thirst for Him. A passionate heart is manifested in the pursuit of the object of its love.

Purged heart

Another characteristic of a heart that is devoted to the Lord is that it is a heart that has been purged of all evil. A heart that has been purged is a heart that is rid of all idols and impurities. God is a holy God, and He demands that our hearts be devoted to Him. You cannot afford to devote to the Lord that which is filled with idols and impurities. When the children of Israel backslid, they asked God for a king and God gave them Saul. When Samuel confronted them, they decided to return to the Lord and this is what he told them, "If you are returning to the LORD with all your hearts, then rid yourselves of the foreign gods and the Ashtoreths and commit yourselves to the LORD and serve him only, and he will deliver you out of the hand of the Philistines" (1Sa 7:3).

Devotion is all about a wholehearted return or commitment to the Lord. And in this verse the old sage prophet of God was giving the people the terms of a total heart commitment to the God of Israel. First he told them to rid themselves of all their idols. This means a heart that is devoted to the Lord has nothing which stands side by side with the Lord. A heart that is totally devoted to the Lord does not only have nothing it values above the Lord, but has nothing it values side by side with the Lord. In other words there is nothing in the life of that individual which competes with the Lord.

For many a Christian, there is nothing that is esteemed more than the Lord. The real problem is that there are many things which compete with the Lord. Many have raised many dagons and set them up beside the Lord in the temple of their hearts. And because dagon can never stand on the same platform like the Lord God Jehovah there are many broken lives and hearts. Are there some things in your heart which compete with your devotion to the God of heaven? Such things might be simple things and commitments that make you unable to give to God the time, energy, finance, and service due Him.

Secondly he asked them to commit themselves to the Lord. In asking them to commit themselves to the Lord Samuel was telling them that in order for them to be devoted to God all that they were and had was to be committed to the Lord. If you are to be devoted to Him, then you must commit yourself totally to the Lord. Your time, your energy, your talents, your money, and all that you are and have. You have to put yourself in a position of no return. You determine in your heart that you are going all the way with God no matter what. Unless you come to this point where you resolve that nothing will keep you from pursuing Him, you cannot qualify as one who is devoted to him.

> *A heart that is totally devoted to the Lord does not only have nothing it values above the Lord, but has nothing it values side by side with the Lord. In other words there is nothing in the life of that individual which competes with the Lord.*

Thirdly, he asked them to serve the Lord only. There are many people serving the Lord, but in serving the Lord they are also serving themselves and their interest. God wants us to serve Him and serve Him only. Some people are serving not the Lord but their religious organizations, ministries, family etc. That is why people are so willing to defend their personal interests even at the expense of the Kingdom of God.

Many people who appear as servants of the Lord today are actually serving their stomachs and building their personal Kingdoms. The truth is that personal kingdoms can only be built at the expense of His one and sovereign Kingdom.

If I may help you probe your own heart, permit me ask you some very straight forward questions: are you serving the Lord or your personal dreams? Are you serving the Lord or some organization? Would you readily embrace that which contradicts your dream if you know for sure that it is what the Lord demands of you? Can you happily serve in a less renowned organization or position? If someone else is asked to lead will you readily follow?

God wants our hearts to be purged of all evil and His Spirit is ready and willing to bring us to the point where our hearts are rid of all idols, our lives are totally committed to Him, and we are serving Him only. You can ask the Holy Spirit to work this out in you.

A heart poured-out to God

Devotion to the Lord is marked by a heart that is poured out to the Lord. By this I am referring to a heart that holds nothing back. It pours all that it is and has in passionate worship to the King of the universe. The Lord so wants our hearts to be totally poured out to Him that He asks us to give our hearts to Him. This is because it is the human tendency to hold back that which it possesses. The only sure way for you to let your heart pour out all it is to God is by giving Him your heart. He says, "My son, give me your heart and let your eyes delight in my ways" (Pr 23:26).

When you respond to this invitation from the Lord, you will realize that your eyes will delight in the ways of the Lord. In other words you will be more interested in knowing the Lord and His ways than in seeing His deeds.

One distinction that was made between Moses and the children of Israel was that the Lord showed His ways to Moses but to the children of Israel, He showed only His deeds. Those whose hearts are held by God are concerned with knowing the ways of the Lord. After all that is what really matters! There are so many people caught up with the deeds of the Lord and have no interest in knowing and understanding His ways. A heart that is devoted to the Lord is a heart that yearns to understand the ways of God. Such a heart is not content with the deeds of the Lord. My friend, you can give God your heart and let your eyes delight in the ways of the Almighty.

> *Are you serving the Lord or some organization? Would you readily embrace that which contradicts your dream if you know for sure that it is what the Lord demands of you? Can you happily serve in a less renowned organization or position? If someone else is asked to lead will you readily follow?*

A poured-out heart is a heart that is marked by obedience to the word of God, it is a heart that will give up anything and hold back nothing from the Lord. It is when our heart is totally poured-out to the Lord that we can serve Him with undivided devotion and refuse the distractions the devil brings to us, because we have become single minded and whole hearted in our service to the King.

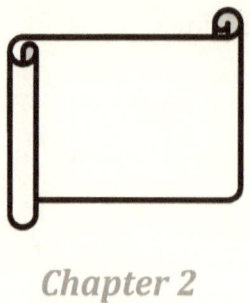

Chapter 2

Dependence

"…and stretch out your hands to him…"

God wants us to stretch out our hands to Him always. I remember we were at an outdoor party some days back and a brother was walking with his one-year old son on the lawn. It seems it was the very first time for this little boy to walk on the lawn and he was having a hard time lifting his feet to make the steps. At a certain point he just stretched out his hands to his daddy who also extended his hands and took the little boy into his arms. I was standing beside them and I said to the father, "is this not what the Lord expects of us?

How often do we reach places where we ought to just stretch out our hands to the Father so He can pick us up and wrap us in His arms, and carry us over the huddles that seem to trip our feet, but because of our arrogance and independence we have held back and suffered unnecessarily!" If we live our lives with outstretched hands to the Lord it shows how dependent we are on Him. "If you would…stretch out your hands to him…" God is looking for men and women whose hands are stretched out so He can shake this world through them.

One of the lessons the Lord is committed to teach us is the lesson of dependence on Him. And the sooner we learn it the better for us. The Lord wants us to totally and completely depend on Him. If we are to qualify as a surrendered people our lives must be in total and complete dependence on the Lord. I like the way the psalmist puts it: "As the eyes of slaves look to the hand of their master, as the eyes of a female slave look to the hand of her mistress, so our eyes look to the LORD our God, till he shows us his mercy" (Ps 123:2).

> God is looking for men and women whose hands are stretched out so He can shake this world through them.

The slave depends totally on his master for instruction, direction, and provision. It only gets what flows from the hands of the master. In the same way the Lord wants us to depend on Him. We are to look to Him for instruction, direction, and provision. Just as the slave takes no independent decision but only what the master decides for him, so we are to depend on the Lord. It is a very difficult thing for us humans to do out of our own free will.

For the slave, he is under compulsion for fear of punishment and abuse by the master. For us it has to come of our own free will. That is what makes it difficult for us to come to such a place where we totally depend on the Lord for every decision we take. The truth is that God is more than willing to help us reach this point in our walk with Him. He knows our greatest fulfillment and satisfaction can only come from a total and complete dependence on Him. And that is what the flesh seeks to keep us from.

One of the greatest counsels I have found in the word is in Proverbs chapter three verses 5-7a: "Trust in the LORD with all your heart and do not lean on your own understanding. In all your ways acknowledge Him, and He will make your paths straight. Do not be wise in your own eyes" (NASB) .

What then is dependence on the Lord?

Not leaning on your understanding

Human initiative is birthed from human understanding of that which is visible. Often such initiatives lead to actions which are independent of God. Our greatest limitation is when we lean on our understanding which can only lead to finite and limited results. The passage above does not say that we should act without understanding but that we should not act based on our own understanding.

Often I have realized that my understanding keeps me in the natural and finite realm. But when I put aside my own understanding and depend on the Lord the results are mind blowing. We so much lean on our own understanding because we fail to trust in the Lord with our whole hearts. That is why the verse begins by exhorting us to trust in the Lord with all our hearts. Once this is done we will cease to depend on our finite understanding and instead submit to the leading of the Holy Spirit.

The Lord wants us to exercise understanding. However, it is not our understanding that He wants us to exercise, but His own understanding. And He seeks to fill us with the Spirit of understanding. Ask the Lord daily to fill you with the Spirit of understanding. I have prayed this prayer for a while now, and increasingly I am ceasing to depend on my human and natural finite understanding but tapping from the infinite understanding of the Spirit. We ought to take conscious decisions to not depend on that which our minds are able to conceive independent of God.

> *Often I have realized that my understanding keeps me in the natural and finite realm. But when I put aside my own understanding and depend on the Lord the results are mind blowing.*

Acknowledging the Lord in all your ways

What does it mean to acknowledge the Lord? I believe it means allowing Him to take the lead, accepting instruction and direction from Him, and acknowledging His infinite knowledge and wisdom. It is giving Him the place He deserves by submitting to His sovereign power and authority. Acknowledging the Lord means you to make any move until you know that He is leading the way. He is the One who knows the ending from the beginning and sees every hurdle or obstacle that lies in the way.

In the book of Isaiah, He promised, "I will lead the blind by ways they have not known, along unfamiliar paths I will guide them; I will turn the darkness into light before them and make the rough places smooth. These are the things I will do; I will not forsake them" (Is 42:16). The truth is that we often dread unknown and unfamiliar paths of life. And it seems that is where the Lord would rather lead us through. And for Him to lead us through we have to follow, and to follow will require depending totally on the Lord. It is like you are on a tour in a place you have never been to. You are forced to depend totally on your tour guide.

In many instances we have been forced to rely on human beings for the direction we need because there was no other option. How much more should we depend on the One who knows all things and never fails? Stepping into the darkness requires depending on the Lord for Him to shine His light and turn the darkness into light. There are many things we will never do or accomplish in life until we come to the point where we are totally, wholly, and completely dependent on the Lord.

Again, He says, "Who among you fears the LORD and obeys the word of his servant? Let the one who walks in the dark, who has no light, trust in the name of the LORD and rely on their God. But now, all you who light fires and provide yourselves with flaming torches go, walk in the light of your fires and of the torches you have set ablaze. This is what you shall receive from my hand: You will lie down in torment" (Is 50:10-11).

Sometimes, even when we are walking in obedience, even when we respond to the word of the Lord from the mouth of His servant, we may still find ourselves in total darkness and uncertainty. At such a point, the enemy has taken advantage of many and has caught them in the web of disillusionment. At this time, you can choose to trust and rely on the Lord, believe His word or light your own fire and take care of the darkness yourself. The Lord exhorts us to choose the former. If you however choose to light your own fire by devising your own schemes, the end result will be torment for your soul. The Lord has promised to turn the darkness we may encounter into light before us. We must exercise patience even when we think the darkness is lasting longer than expected. Acknowledging the Lord means staying put until He shines His light. Now this is dependence!

> There are many things we will never do or accomplish in life until we come to the point where we are totally, wholly, and completely dependent on the Lord.

May the Lord by His tender mercies bring us to a point of total dependence so that we can enjoy its fruits, some of which are that our paths will be made straight and the rough places made smooth. Isn't that glorious? It pays to depend on the Lord, and the wise at heart refuse to depend on their own understanding.

Do not be wise in your own eyes

Human wisdom was given us by the Lord but it can never and should never replace divine wisdom in the life of a believer. Wisdom is the right application of knowledge. However in the realm where we are called to operate as believers, human wisdom only amounts to folly. What we need is the Spirit of wisdom, which is the wisdom of the Lord God. The Lord wants us to rise to the level of operating in divine wisdom. But we can only get there when we refuse to be wise in our own eyes or to trust even our most acute judgment or decision taken independent of Him.

Reckless abandon

Another way by which our independence from the Lord is manifested is in our tendency to defend ourselves and fight for our rights. In defending ourselves we often turn to ungodly means, ungodly behavior, and compromise. If we are dependent on the Lord we leave Him to vindicate and defend us when the need arises. We see this several times in the life of David who refused to defend himself against those who assailed him. He entrusted himself to the Lord and allowed the Lord to determine the outcome of the attacks on his reputation and authority.

There is one other story of dependence on the Lord manifested in reckless abandon. It is the story of the Hebrew lads in Babylon who were to be killed if they did not worship the king's idol. Their dependence on the Lord was manifested in a reckless abandon to the Lord. Just read what they told the king of Babylon after he threatened them with incineration in a seven times- hot furnace:

"Shadrach, Meshach and Abednego replied to him, "King Nebuchadnezzar, we do not need to defend ourselves before you in this matter. [17] If we are thrown into the blazing furnace, the God we serve is able to deliver us from it, and he will deliver us from Your Majesty's hand. [18] But even if he does not, we want you to know, Your Majesty, that we will not serve your gods or worship the image of gold you have set up" (Dan 3:16-17). Because of their dependence on the Lord they refused to defend themselves before the King. They were willing to lay down their lives if the Lord would not intervene on their behalf.

In defending ourselves, we often turn to ungodly means, ungodly behavior, and compromise. If we are dependent on the Lord we leave Him to vindicate and defend us when the need arises.

How many times have we compromised because we did not depend on the Lord? My friend, dependence requires a reckless abandonment in the hands of the Lord. For those who truly depend on the Lord, external pressure or change in circumstances means nothing and will never push them from their platform of dependence on Him.

Our supreme example

To have a deeper understanding of what dependence really is, we have to look at the life of the Lord Jesus. No one else has manifested dependence on the Father like the Son when He was on earth and even now in glory. His dependence was whole, total, and complete in every sense of the word. Our Lord depended on the Father for what He was to say or do, and how He was to say or do it; and we have been called to follow in His footsteps of dependence on the Father for everything and in everything.

The simple truth is that, many of us are greatly limited, if not totally paralyzed by our independence and tendency to act on what we know or have experienced in the past. Your degree of effectiveness in the Kingdom is directly proportional to your degree of dependence on the God of heaven. The following verses give you a picture of our Lord's dependence on the Father. Is there any doubt He accomplished in less than four years what will take us eternity to grasp?

'Therefore Jesus answered and was saying to them, "Truly, truly, I say to you, the Son can do nothing of Himself, unless it is something He sees the Father doing; for whatever the Father does, these things the Son also does in like manner"' (Jn 5:19).

"I have much to say in judgment of you. But he who sent me is trustworthy, and what I have heard from him I tell the world" (Jn 8:26).

"I know that his command leads to eternal life. So whatever I say is just what the Father has told me to say" (Jn 12:50).

If we copy the dependence of our precious Lord and Savior, we will accomplish far more in the shortest possible time than all our mechanisms of independence can in several lifetimes.

Chapter 3

Decided Sanctification

"If you put away the sin that is in your hand…"

There is a sanctification that took place in our lives when we came to the Lord in repentance. There is also a sanctification that comes automatically as we expose our hearts to the word of God and walk in the light and fellowship of the saints. The Bible says,

"And that is what some of you were. But you were washed, you were sanctified, you were justified in the name of the Lord Jesus Christ and by the Spirit of our God" (1Co 6:11).

"If we claim to have fellowship with him and yet walk in the darkness, we lie and do not live out the truth. But if we walk in the light, as he is in the light, we have fellowship with one another, and the blood of Jesus, his Son, purifies us from all sin" (1Jn 1:6-7).

"Husbands, love your wives, even as Christ also loved the church, and gave himself for it; That he might sanctify and cleanse it with the washing of water by the word" (Eph 5:4-5).

As we walk in the light

As we walk in the light of the revelation given us by the Spirit, as our hearts respond to the word of God, the Holy Spirit carries out a cleansing work in us for those sins we may never be aware of. This is how the word washes us. Remember what David said, "But who can discern their own errors? Forgive my hidden faults. Keep your servant also from willful sins; may they not rule over me. Then I will be blameless, innocent of great transgression" (Ps 19:12-13).

David is saying there are some errors that are impossible for us to discern, especially when it comes to motives and intents. He calls them hidden faults. These are the ones we are cleansed from as we expose ourselves to the word of the Lord, and respond to the light of revelation. They are sins which were not willful or presumptuous. It is because of this cleansing power of the word and of fellowship with the saints that a man may be regarded blameless by the Lord. When John wrote his epistle and said, "If we claim to have no sin we make Him to be a liar", he was referring to these unpresumptuous sins. This sanctifying work of the word and of our fellowship with the Spirit is what I call undecided sanctification-we automatically benefit from it as we walk with the Lord.

The role of our wills

There is however, what I call decided sanctification, which is a heart commitment to get rid of, and to abandon all known sin. Verse 14a, of our passage in Job 11 says, "if you will put away the sin that is in your hand…" This is a conscious decision and determination to deal a fatal blow to the sins that beset us. It stems from the will of a man in response to the convicting power of the Holy Spirit.

The sins of the hand are the sins that a man makes a conscious decision to commit. Therefore there needs to be a conscious decision to deal with it and make things right with the Lord. Just reading the word and fellowshipping with the saints does not bring cleansing from willful sins. At best it will bring conviction, and it's our respond to conviction that brings sanctification. This comes only from a conscious decision to walk in sanctification. James in writing to the saints said, "Come near to God and he will come near to you. Wash your hands, you sinners, and purify your hearts, you double-minded." (Jas 4:8).

In the above verse James appeals to the will of the people to draw near to the Lord and asks them to wash their hands and purify their hearts. He was asking them to make a decision to be sanctified and to walk in holiness. This is where devotion comes in; we cannot truly talk of devotion to the Lord if we are not committed to deal with all known sin and to walk in holiness. Our degree of devotion is manifested in the degree to which we are uncomfortable with any form of sin in our lives and our conscious efforts to cleanse our hearts by the power of the blood of Jesus.

Have you come to the point where you call sin by its name and refuse to provide a dwelling place for it in the temple of your body and the altar of the heart? If you have, then devotion is within reach for you. And remember to properly deal with sin will require confession, repentance, cleansing, and where possible, restitution. It will take the power of the Holy Spirit from beginning to end to go through the process of dealing with sin and entering a life of decided sanctification. It is something worth the pursuit so go for it and stop at nothing!

A passion to be searched

David was so committed to living a sanctified life that he prayed often, asking the Lord to search his heart and expose any sin to him so he could repent of it. If we devote ourselves to the Lord and decide to live a sanctified life, we must engage the searching light of the Holy Spirit to expose any darkness and sin in order for us to deal with it permanently. To live as though everything is always right is to live in presumption. And there is no greater prison than that of presumptuousness. It blinds your eyes to the reality of God's holiness and justice. Like David, pray on a regular basis asking the Lord to search your heart and make known to you anything that is displeasing to Him.

David started Psalm 139 by saying, "You have searched me, Lord, and you know me" (v1), and ended it with a prayer saying, "Search me, God, and know my heart; test me and know my anxious thoughts. See if there is any offensive way in me, and lead me in the way everlasting" (vv 23-24). This shows us that he constantly brought his life under the scrutiny of the holy presence of Adonai. Those who live a decided sanctified life are those who trust not themselves but the Lord and long to see Him approve the conditions of their heart.

> *If we devote ourselves to the Lord and decide to live a sanctified life, we must engage the searching light of the Holy Spirit to expose any darkness and sin in order for us to deal with it permanently. To live as though everything is always right is to live in presumption. And there is no greater prison than that of presumptuousness*

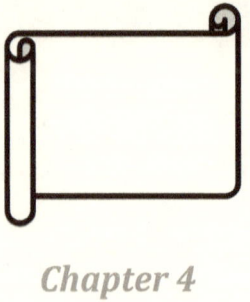

Chapter 4

Determined Consecration

"...and allow no evil to dwell in your tent..."

Another requisite for a surrendered life is a life that is consecrated to the Lord. The word tent here can refer to the body or the house we live in. Whatever the case consecration means we allow no evil to dwell in the tent of our body or home. Determined consecration means we see our bodies and the environment in which we dwell as sacred unto the Lord. It is this state of holy consciousness of the sacredness of all that we are and have that makes us yield to the workings of the Holy Spirit in us and through us.

The tent of your body

Your body is the tent in which the real you lives. And this tent has many gateways through which intruders can get in and cause harm. Just as the house in which you live has many entrances through which thieves can enter and you do all to keep them closed and protected, so you must watch over the gates of the tent of your body to keep evil from entering and dwelling there. The Lord requires you to "offer your bodies as living sacrifices, holy and pleasing to God" (Ro 12:1). And you can't afford to offer Him a body in which evil dwells.

Guarding your tent

> *Determined consecration means we see our bodies and the environment in which we dwell as sacred unto the Lord. It is this state of holy consciousness of the sacredness of all that we are and have that makes us yield to the workings of the Holy Spirit in us and through us.*

For evil to dwell in the body, it must first of all gain entrance. And once evil has entrenched itself in a place, it takes a lot more effort to have it uprooted. The best way to deal with evil is to keep it out and allow it no passage way. This can be effectively done by keeping watch over the different gates into the human body and soul which include the eyes, ears, hands, feet, and other passage ways.

When the Lord says you should guard your heart above all else (see Pr 4:23), he is asking you to beware of what goes through the gates of your tent. For everything that enters your tent will ultimately seek to establish itself in the heart. The secret to ward off such intruders is to build a garrison round your heart, by building fortresses at the gates of the human soul and body. And if by chance because of negligence you allow anything to gain entrance in the tent of His habitation, you will not hesitate for a moment to throw it out.

The tent of your body is the Temple of the Holy Spirit. It is your responsibility to ensure that the temple is in the right condition. Like backslidden Israel, many of us have erected idols and allow other abominable elements to inhabit His dwelling place. We have even offered a room to strangers to dwell in the temple of the Lord as some leaders did in the time of the rebuilding. The solution is to carry out a campaign of purification.

Purifying the Temple

Our reference passage here is II Chronicles 29. Hezekiah came to the throne of Israel, taking over from his father who had caused Israel to backslide. The temple of the Lord in Jerusalem was in a state of dilapidation, desecration, and decay. The doors of the Temple had been closed, temple worship abandoned, and of course the presence of the Lord had left because His dwelling place had been neglected. Immediately he came to the throne of Israel, Hezekiah began a work to restore the temple worship in the nation and the first thing he did was to purify the Temple of the Lord.

Permit me ask: what is the state of the temple of your body? Is it fit for worship and for habitation by Jehovah?

The first thing Hezekiah did was to open and repair the doors of the temple that had been closed. This is the starting point of consecration. You have to open the doors of your life which have been closed to the light of the Spirit and the word. Many people's lives are totally closed to the Holy Spirit. There are portions of their temple they would not allow the Holy Spirit access. They have kept the word of God out of those areas of their lives. Friend, open the doors of your life for the Holy Spirit and the light of His word to come in and expel the darkness that has made its habitation therein.

You must understand that when you open the doors of your tent to evil you automatically close it to the glory of His presence. The quickest way to put God out is to deliberately bring in evil. Open every door and let in the light. Open the doors to your hurts and disappointments. Open the doors to you fears and misgivings. Open the doors to your secret sins. Open the doors to your doubts and uncertainties. Open the doors to your broken relationships. Open every door and ask the Holy Spirit to shine His light into that part of your heart which had been closed to Him until now. Let His light shine in so you can see the strange things which are there and take them out. Hezekiah also repaired the doors which though closed to the light of His presence were open to the darkness of evil. You will have to repair the doors of your heart and put out evil in all its manifestations.

Secondly, he removed all defilement from the Temple. He did not remove the defilements before repairing the doors because he understood that when the doors are in shambles any evil you drive out will come back right in. So he took the time and the pains to repair the doors first. Once he had repaired the doors, he now removed the defilement out of the temple. Because the doors were in place the defilement could stay out of the temple.

Take a look at the temple of the Holy Spirit which is the tent of your body. Is there anything in it and on it that is causing defilement? It is time to take it out: anger, bitterness, hatred, jealousy, slander, hypocrisy, duplicity, dissent, impure thoughts, impurity, sexual immorality, falsehood and the rest. These are the things which defile the temple. And if you must purify the temple you have no choice but to take them out.

Thirdly, they consecrated the Temple of the Lord. That which is consecrated to the Lord is given for the exclusive use for the glory of the Lord. That is why Paul exhorted us saying, "Therefore, I urge you, brothers and sisters, in view of God's mercy, to offer your bodies as a living sacrifice, holy and pleasing to God—this is your true and proper worship" (Ro 12:1). However you can't rush to this step if you have neglected the first two.

The tent of your habitation

Having looked at how to consecrate the tent of His habitation which is your body, we now turn to the tent of your habitation which is your home and environment. It is not enough to have your body consecrated and have it dwell in a defiling environment. Remember, both the courts of the temple and the temple itself had to be purified. Your home is the courts of the temple (your body). For consecration to be total, the courts also have to be cleansed and purified. You must take away anything questionable including movies, music and any item that may be a landing spot for Satan and his agents. Consecrate the temple and make it fit for the extension of His glory. Let your consecration be determined from your heart, and then you will be on the pathway to total surrender.

> *You must understand that when you open the doors of your tent to evil, you automatically close it to the glory of His presence. The quickest way to put God out is to deliberately bring in evil.*

Chapter 5

Dead to Gain

"…and assign your nuggets to the dust, your gold of Ophir to the rocks in the ravines…"

The love, desire, and pursuit of gain constitute a great obstacle to a life of total surrender. The love of gain has killed dreams, grounded destinies, destroyed lives, and wrecked ministries. The Lord God wants us to prosper and be blessed in every way possible, but He doesn't want our love to be exercised towards gain. If you want to live a life of absolute surrender and enjoy of its fruits, you must die to gain; financial gain, material gain, social gain, etc.

The rich young ruler

The story of the rich young ruler in the Bible is a perfect example of how the love of gain can prevent one from totally surrendering to the Lord of glory. He had seen his need for a Savior, though he had been living in righteousness according to the law. When he came to Christ Jesus and asked Him what he needed to do to inherit eternal life, the Lord told him to sell all he had and give the money to the poor. By saying this, the Lord was pointing out his need for total and absolute surrender. Jesus was saying if he could die to gain and worldly riches, he would truly, unreservedly follow Him.

> The Lord God wants us to prosper and be blessed in every way possible, but He doesn't want our love to be exercised towards gain. If you want to live a life of absolute surrender and enjoy of its fruits, you must die to gain; financial gain, material gain, social gain, etc.

In a sense, only surrendered people can truly follow and serve the Lord. Hence the Lord wanted him to meet the requisite of a surrendered life which he lacked. But the sad thing is that the Bible tells us he was saddened by this request and went away. He was not ready to meet the requisite of a surrendered life, and therefore walked away from the blessings that come only through absolute surrender. The problem was not his riches but his refusal to surrender his right to those riches that acted as a barrier to his entry into the kingdom.

My dear friend, you need to surrender your treasure and all your gain to the Lord. You have to lay them at His feet, for His use and the expansion of His kingdom. I am not asking you to go sell all you have and give to the poor. I am saying you have to place all within the reach of the Lord, that He may use it as He sees fit. This is what dead to gain is all about: taking a disposition of obedience to make use of all you have and are as the Lord leads. This is not limited to financial, material, or monetary gain. It simply means the things you value and hold in esteem. It may be your education, position, relationship, profession or anything which can be considered your gold of Ophir.

Part two:

The battles and struggles of surrender

Because of the great blessings that come as a result of surrendering to the Lord, the satanic trinity (the devil, the world, and the flesh) does everything to resist and prevent us from taking this determinant step of total surrender. Everyone who ever came to a point of total surrender to the Lord will acknowledge the struggles and battles that are involved. The outcome of each of these struggles determines how soon we reach the point of absolute surrender. And even after we have reached that point, it takes another whole level of battles or struggles to stay surrendered. In this section, we will look at some of the obstacles to total surrender and see how we can overcome them. I have realized that the best way to learn is to look at the lives of Bible characters and allow the Spirit of God to use them as a mirror for us to see our own lives through.

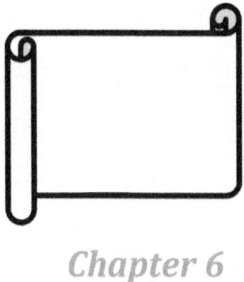

Chapter 6

Fear

Fear is one of the greatest obstacles to absolute surrender. Usually our fears are disguised into spiritual languages, cultural beliefs, medical terminologies, and ideological and philosophical concepts to which we have given mental accent. Fears are the most subtle enemies to the progress of mankind. Usually it appears as though your fears are making you safe and secure but they can only give you apparent safety while keeping you from taking a more rewarding risk.

There is no greater danger in life than decay; and what fear does is that it keeps you from functioning and moving forward. This lack of progressive motion opens the way for decay. Many people have decaying dreams, potentials, gifts, and talents because they have allowed themselves to be engulfed and chained down in a cocoon of fear. You cannot allow yourself to be engulfed in a cocoon of fear without suffering from its paralyzing effect. What are some of the ways in which fear manifests itself?

Fear of the future

The future God has planned for you is bright beyond your wildest dreams. But to get there you have to take risks and be willing to move into it. The Bible says "no one can discover anything about their future" (Ecc 7:14b). This impossibility to discover one's future makes many people to fear, doubt, and dread what it holds. But if you have faith in God you know that the best future is reserved for you. You believe Him and leap into where He is leading you. Faith for the future makes you bold and courageous to face it, knowing that the One who has the future in His hands, has you too In His hands.

So to overcome this fear of the future, you have to come in agreement with God's word, that all it says concerning your future will come to reality as you believe Him and take the little steps of faith required to activate the future.

Fear of the unknown and the unfamiliar

Fear of the unknown and the unfamiliar is very closely related to fear of the future. However, they are different because the unknown and the unfamiliar do not necessarily have to do with the future. Sometimes fear of the unknown has to do just with the opportunities which present themselves before us in life. And only those who are willing to face the unfamiliar dare to accept such opportunities.

As a result of Peter's unwillingness to deal with the unfamiliar he almost lost the opportunity to take the gospel of Jesus to the gentiles. If you are to surrender to the Lord, it will require you to be willing and ready to face the unknown, the uncertain, and the unfamiliar. To overcome this manifestation of fear, you need to trust the Lord who has promised to lead you and to guide you with His eye. The fact that such opportunities are unknown and unfamiliar means they can take you, if exploited, into unknown and unfamiliar heights and spheres of influence with God and with man.

Fear of man and systems

This is another dangerous obstacle and snare that lurks ever closer, seeking to get an ever increasing grip on its victim. Fear of man is the most subtle

> *Usually it appears as though your fears are making you safe and secure but they can only give you apparent safety while keeping you from taking a more rewarding risk.*

and most common manifestation of fear because we all are surrounded by men and women who seek to control and intimidate us directly or indirectly. Why this form of fear has a greater capacity to subtly paralyze is because of man's tendency to belong and to be accepted by other men. Fear of man gives birth to the fear of rejection and inflates the insecurity that lies within.

To deal with the fear of man, you and I must deal with our insecurities, knowing that God is able to give us the right company that will support our dreams and make us fulfill the destiny He has for us. That is why it so important to lay all your relationships at the foot of the cross, and allow the Holy Spirit to strip you off those that will become a hindrance to God's plan for your life which can be fulfilled only through absolute surrender.

Fear of failure

Fear of failure grips us when we trust in our own strength, gifts, talents, abilities, or capabilities. When we come face to face with challenges that are obviously greater than our abilities, the result is to avoid trying because of the fear to fail. In life, the Lord will lead you to do things which are far beyond your gifting, talents, or abilities. At such times, He stretches you to tap from His infinite reservoir of strength and all you may need. The Lord wants us to trust in Him and depend on that which He can do through us. And it takes confidence in the Lord to be able to face that which is obviously bigger or stronger than you. Success comes from favor before the Lord and not from your abilities, so cease to depend on the latter and allow the Lord to work through you. Then you shall be amazed at what He is able to do through your frailty.

> Usually our fears are disguised into spiritual languages, cultural beliefs, medical terminologies, and ideological and philosophical concepts to which we have given mental accent.

See what it did to them

The first example of how the fear of man can prevent someone from surrendering to what he knows is the will of God is that of king Zedekiah. The Lord sent the Babylonian army to besiege Judah because the people were unfaithful and had abandoned the ways of the Lord. The king inquired from the prophet Jeremiah whether it was God's will to go to battle and the prophet did not hesitate to let him know that surrender was the only option the Lord was giving them. Suddenly the king found himself in an imbroglio of surrendering to a heathen king especially when his officials wanted otherwise.

Often the will of the Lord will come in conflict with what others think should be, and we are left with the choice of whether to obey the Lord or to succumb to the ever present pressure to please those around us. Of course Zedekiah refused to obey the Lord because of his fear of man, and this led to his death (Jer 38:14-28).

The next example of the danger of the fear of man is in the story of King Saul. He had received a command from the Lord to go destroy the Amalekites together with all they had. Of course Saul did not totally obey this order from the Commander of the hosts of heaven. When confronted by the prophet Samuel, this is what Saul said, "Then Saul said to Samuel, "I have sinned. I violated the LORD's command and your instructions. I was afraid of the men and so I gave in to them" (1Sa15:24). The fear of man is truly a snare that will entangle you and strangle the life out of you. It will cause you to give in when you are supposed to refuse, abandon when you are supposed to pursue, run when you are supposed to stand, and resist when you are supposed to submit. This was exactly the case with Saul.

Do not allow the fear of man to keep you from fulfilling your destiny as it did king Saul. The secret to overcoming the fear of man is to allow yourself to be filled and possessed with the fear of the Lord. Someone has rightly said that he who fears God has no fear of man. The fear of God not only keeps you from sinning against Him but helps you escape from the snare set for you by the fear of man. Let your heart delight in the fear of the Lord, it is the secret to overcoming all other fears.

> *To deal with the fear of man, you and I must deal with our insecurities, knowing that God is able to give us the right company that will support our dreams and make us fulfill the destiny He has for us.*

Chapter 7

Self-initiative

Initiative in itself is not bad, but like any good thing, it can also stand on the way of our surrendering to, and embracing the will of God. Sometimes, if not every time, our initiatives result from our personal likes or dislikes, our inclinations and propensities, biases and prejudices. And the basic truth is that anything which originates from the will of man, even redeemed man, will often be in conflict with the will of God. But when we delight in Him, and come to the place of surrender, He works out His will through us such that it seems as though we were the ones taking the initiative or making the decision.

This is the point where Paul found himself when he wrote: "I have been crucified with Christ and I no longer live, but Christ lives in me. The life I now live in the body, I live by faith in the Son of God, who loved me and gave himself for me" (Gal 2:20). And this is the kind of life the Father wants us to live. But to get here we must lay down our self-initiatives as soon as we realize they are in conflict with the divine will for our lives.

I should not be misunderstood as saying that our initiatives have no place in our service to the Lord. However, they must be regenerated by laying them on the cross for crucifixion. When we crucify our initiatives and allow the Holy Spirit to breathe life and resurrection power into them, they become a mighty tool to bring to existence unparalleled visions and dreams that will bring heaven to earth, and move the hearts of men back to the God of heaven.

> When we crucify our initiatives and allow the Holy Spirit to breathe life and resurrection power into them, they become a mighty tool to bring to existence unparalleled visions and dreams that will bring heaven to earth, and move the hearts of men back to the God of heaven.

There is a prayer Paul made for the Church in Thessalonica in his second epistle to them. He said, "With this in mind, we constantly pray for you, that our God may make you worthy of his calling, and that by his power he may bring to fruition your every desire for goodness and your every deed prompted by faith. We pray this so that the name of our Lord Jesus may be glorified in you, and you in him, according to the grace of our God and the Lord Jesus Christ" (2Th 1:11-12). What a prayer!

Can you imagine that your every desire for goodness is brought to fruition? This is the place the Lord wants us to dwell in, where all our desires for goodness are granted. What a fulfilled life the Lord wants us to live. But this can only happen after we delight in the Lord. When we take delight in Him, He places His desires in our hearts and we begin to desire what He wills and by so doing we give Him the pleasure of fulfilling those desires.

Remember the exhortation of the psalmist to "Take delight in the LORD, and he will give you the desires of your heart" (Ps 37:4). Paul prayed that God may bring to fruition not only the desire for goodness but also every deed prompted by the faith of the Thessalonians. Think about that for a moment! Every deed prompted by their faith? Wow! It is amazing to see where the Spirit of God wants us to be as saints. But the key to this is death to every initiative from the flesh.

Learning from history

The Son of God, (God the Son) said He did nothing of His own accord but only what was initiated by the Father. He saw what the Father was doing and followed suit. I want you to know that He made the statement as the Son of Man, that is, omnipotence and omniscience clothed in the tent of human frailty. He was without sin, and all that preceded from Him was absolute perfection. Yet He refused to take any initiative but followed the Father's lead.

David the man after God's heart got into trouble several times because he took some initiatives and did not inquire from the Lord. When he took an initiative to transport the Ark of the Covenant without asking how it should be done, he got into trouble. When he took the initiative to number the fighting men in the nation of Israel, he got into trouble.

Saul also who lost it because he took the initiative to spare the best cattle of the Amalekites in order to sacrifice them to the Lord meanwhile the Lord had commanded him to have everything destroyed. Every initiative that stems from the flesh will only lead us to the path of conflict with the will of God. But if it stems from the Spirit of God we are sure that it will lead to a blessing for all involved.

Chapter 8

Self-will

Self-will is another great obstacle to the life of total surrender. Self-will is very strongly related to self-initiative but has to do with our resolve to be the master of our own lives. This is manifested in the inability to yield to the will of another. As examples, I would like us to consider how self-will manifested in the life of two of the foremost apostles in the early church; Peter and Paul.

Peter's Arrogance

Self-will can make someone to fail to take warning when necessary to avert a situation that can be prevented. On the eve of the Lord's crucifixion, he had revealed that the devil had asked to sieve Peter from the fold, and that this was going to manifest in Peter's denial of Him. However, instead of Peter taking heed to the warning and humbly praying that this should not be the case, Peter objected the Lord by stating how self-determined he was to even die for the Lord. "Peter replied, "Even if all fall away on account of you, I never will." "Truly I tell you," Jesus answered, "this very night, before the rooster crows, you will disown me three times." But Peter declared, "Even if I have to die with you, I will never disown you." And all the other disciples said the same" (Mt 26:33-35).

Here, Peter's self-will for martyrdom was a great hindrance to his surrendering to the Lord and praying that he would be able to find grace to stand the trial that was coming his way. Have we not spent time arguing with the Lord where we should just have submitted and taken our place in prayer? Is it not wisdom when we give in to the One who knows the end from the beginning and knows the outcome of every trial? We know that if the Lord did not pray for Peter, it would have been a totally devastating situation when Peter finally disowned Him. Who knows what his remorse would have done? May be like Judah it could have ended up in suicide. For, not many people are able to stand the guilt and condemnation that comes as a result of betrayal.

How it got Paul in trouble

Paul was known for his strong self-will and of course this stood on his way to total surrender to the Lord. Due to this strong self-will, he argued with the Lord when He asked him to leave Jerusalem in Acts 22: 17-21. Many years after, He decided to return to Jerusalem. The Holy Spirit was not in accord with this journey as He spoke through a group of believers but again Paul would not listen because he was bent (self-will) on taking the gospel to the Jews of Jerusalem. This is a summary of what happened:

"We sought out the disciples there and stayed with them seven days. Through the Spirit they urged Paul not to go on to Jerusalem. When it was time to leave, we left and continued on our way. All of them, including wives and children, accompanied us out of the city, and there on the beach we knelt to pray. After saying goodbye to each other, we went aboard the ship, and they returned home…After we had been there a number of days, a prophet named Agabus came down from Judea. Coming over to us, he took Paul's belt, tied his own hands and feet with it and said, "The Holy Spirit says, 'In this way the Jewish leaders in Jerusalem will bind the owner of this belt and will hand him over to the Gentiles.'" When we heard this, we and the people there pleaded with Paul not to go up to Jerusalem. Then Paul answered, "Why are you weeping and breaking my heart? I am ready not only to be bound, but also to die in Jerusalem for the name of the Lord Jesus." When he would not be dissuaded, we gave up and said, "The Lord's will be done." After this, we started on our way up to Jerusalem." (Acts 21:4-6, 10-15)

Clearly, the Holy Spirit wanted to stop Paul from going to Jerusalem, but his willingness to die for the Lord was to strong that he could not be dissuaded.. It is true that through his arrest in Jerusalem, he was able to sail to Rome and take the gospel there with him. However, I believe the Holy Spirit had another path for him. Because of the Lord's grace and mercy, He was able to use this episode in Paul's life for good as He did for Peter. But they both missed the blessings that would have come with their surrendering. It is written, *"The prudent see danger and take refuge, but the simple keep going and pay the penalty (Pr 27:12).* Let us be known as the prudent ones, not those who persist because of self-will and suffer unnecessarily!

This list of struggles and obstacles to the surrendered life is not by any means exhaustive; I only treated the most common and most subtle obstacles. Each person's experience will be different and unique in its own way.

Part 3:

The Rewards or Blessings of a Surrendered Life

In the first two parts we have looked at what qualifies us for the blessings of a surrendered life, namely; the requirements or requisites for a surrendered life which we treated in part one, and the struggles and battles of surrender which we treated in part two. In this part, we are going to look at the blessings of a surrendered life which come on us when we have met the requirements of total surrender. The good thing is that even while we may still be in the battle and struggles for surrender, we can reap the blessings that God has designed for those who go the way of total surrender. The simple truth is that we are all in this battle for total surrender, just that some may be closer the place of absolute surrender than others, but we all still have battles. The Lord is interested in our desire for total surrender and our determination to pay the price. So what then are the results, benefits, or blessings of surrender?

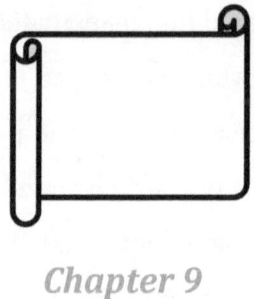

Chapter 9

Confidence

"…then, free of fault, you will lift up your face…"

One of the blessings of a surrendered life is confidence. One translation puts the above portion as, '…then, you will lift up your face without shame…" The Lord wants us to live without shame of our past or of our current weaknesses and shortcomings, or of our failures. People who live in shame walk around with their heads bowed. They look down when talking to those they consider themselves inferior to. However when you are filled with confidence, you walk tall. You are ready to confront challenges and face difficulties without any trepidation.

A lesson from David

The psalmist said,

"The LORD is my light and my salvation— whom shall I fear? The LORD is the stronghold of my life— of whom shall I be afraid? When the wicked advance against me to devour me, it is my enemies and my foes who will stumble and fall. Though an army besiege me, my heart will not fear; though war break out against me, even then I will be confident" (Ps 27:1-2).

> *When we are surrendered to the Lord we come to the point where we are confident to walk even in the dark as long as we are sure He is in the lead.*

This is a statement that portrays utmost confidence. David knew the Lord as his light and his salvation. This means he was confident the Lord would shine in the midst of any darkness he may encounter. He was sure that no darkness would surround him without the Lord who was his light breaking through and lighting the way for him. When we are surrendered to the Lord we come to the point where we are confident to walk even in the dark as long as we are sure He is in the lead.

David also knew the Lord as his salvation and so he was confident that there could be no situation from which the Lord would not save him. Surrender brings us to a point where we are unafraid to face any danger because we know the One who is leading us is able to bring us salvation whenever there is need. When we deal with our fears, we receive a revelation of the Lord as the light and salvation of our lives.

He also knew the Lord as the stronghold of his life. We arrive at this point when we realize that we are incapable of defending ourselves against men or against the powers of evil arrayed against us. It takes a surrendered person to allow the Lord to be his defense especially against those he is stronger than. But we see it so often in the life of David; he refused to defend himself even against those he could have slain in the twinkling of an eye.

Because he knew the Lord was the stronghold of his life he let everything be decided by God. He was confident in the protection heaven offered him. The truth is, unless the Lord protects us, all the protection and self-defense mechanisms we generate will amount to nothing. Because of his confidence in the Lord's protection he was able to proclaim that all who attacked him were going to stumble. Now, that is real confidence. The capacity to stay calm and focused even with tens of thousands of enemy troops gathered around him to take his life, could only be given to the one who has made considerable progress in the school of absolute surrender.

If you were besieged by an army of problems and trials, would you still be confident that the Lord will keep you safe? In the midst of conflict and strife will you be confident, knowing that the Lord can never and will never lose a battle? Why is surrender a condition for one to have this kind of confidence? The simple reason is that only those who have laid down their lives on the altar of the Lord can be ready and willing to engage in any battle for the sole sake of the Kingdom and the glory. Confidence in God is a result of absolute surrender.

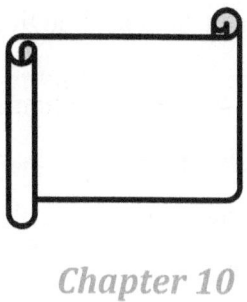

Chapter 10

Stability

"…you will stand firm…"

Another great benefit of absolute surrender is the blessing of stability; the ability to stand firm, unmoved by circumstances and external variation and changes. Those who have taken a firm stand in the Lord and against sin and other practices have reached a point of surrender. They are not afraid of the outcome of the judgment of men. Instability in faith, beliefs, confessions, and professions are all a result of not having surrendered to the Lord in totality. As such, people's beliefs, confessions, and professions change as the external circumstances change to their favor or disfavor.

Until you come to the point of total surrender, your life will be like a reed swayed by the wind. Surrender is what brings you to the point where you are "No longer infants, tossed back and forth by the waves, and blown here and there by every wind of teaching and by the cunning and craftiness of people in their deceitful scheming" (Eph 4:14). I have seen people who have no clear position about very important issues of life.

Their position depends on who is saying what. Year in, year out I have seen them turning about the same spot as though enjoying being swayed.

Some people are like simple pendulums, moving back and forth without making any reasonable progress or change of position. They are executing motion and expending energy yet making no progress. This too, is a result of instability. God expects us to make measurable translational progress in our Christian life towards the accomplishment of our destiny. And surrender is what enables us to make such progress. Men will invent schemes of deceit to remove you from a secure position. The only way you can survive the deluge of schemes of men who intend to deceive you and those who may be sincerely mistaken, is to stand firm. And stability is an offspring of surrender.

Why do you need to stand firm?
Standing firm determines your victory

The outcome of the battles you will face in life depends on whether you are standing firm or not. Here are some scriptural exhortations on the need to stand firm and what it results to:

- *It will bring you triumph over the enemy*: "Moses answered the people, "Do not be afraid. Stand firm and you will see the deliverance the LORD will bring you today. The Egyptians you see today you will never see again" (Ex 14:13).

- *It will bring you deliverance from your enemies*: "You will not have to fight this battle. Take up your positions; stand firm and see the deliverance the LORD will give you, Judah and Jerusalem. Do not be afraid; do not be discouraged. Go out to face them tomorrow, and the LORD will be with you" (2Ch 20:17).

- *It guarantees your salvation*: "You will be hated by everyone because of me, but the one who stands firm to the end will be saved" (Mt 10:22).

- *It will make you fully devoted to the work of the Lord*: "Therefore, my dear brothers and sisters, stand firm. Let nothing move you. Always give yourselves fully to the work of the Lord, because you know that your labor in the Lord is not in vain" (1Co 15:58).

- *It keeps you free*: "It is for freedom that Christ has set us free. Stand firm, then, and do not let yourselves be burdened again by a yoke of slavery" (Gal 5:1).

> *The only way you can survive the deluge of schemes of men who intend to deceive you and those who may be sincerely mistaken, is to stand firm. And stability is an offspring of surrender.*

The Lord wants you to reach a place where you are firmly planted like a tree in the vineyard of the Lord; firm, secure, and unaffected by anything.

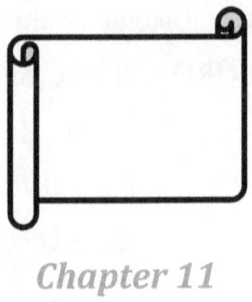

Chapter 11

Boldness

"…and without fear…"

In part two of our study we talked of fear as an obstacle to absolute surrender. And we saw how we could deal with the different manifestations of self. Once we set out to deal with our fears, the Lord enables us to overcome them by the power of His Spirit and to live and serve without any form of fear. You ask if it is possible to live without fear. Absolutely! One of the prophecies made about the Messiah was that He was "to rescue us from the hand of our enemies, and to enable us to serve him without fear" (Lk 1:74).

God is in the business of making His sons and daughters serve Him without fear, even in the midst of the most severe threats. He wants to bring us to the place of boldness and intrepidity. This is the place of the fullness of blessing in the life of a believer. It is possible to be totally free from any form of fear. The Bible says fear brings torments and we know that torments steal away joy and hope from its victim. The Lord wants us to be free from all forms of fear, overt or covert, so we can exhibit the contaminating joy of the Lord to the whole world. When we live without fear, we will enjoy the abundant life that the Lord Jesus came for us to have.

> God is in the business of making His sons and daughters serve Him without fear, even in the midst of the most severe threats. He wants to bring us to the place of boldness and intrepidity.

Let it take possession of you

The Bible says "For God did not give us a spirit of timidity (of cowardice, of craven and cringing and fawning fear), but [He has given us a spirit] of power and of love and of calm and well-balanced mind and discipline and self-control." (2Ti 1:7, Amp) Power, a calm and well-balanced mind, and love are all elements of the boldness that God gives when we decide to deal with our fears. In fact God has already given us this spirit of boldness. What you have to do is to let it flow and take possession of your whole being by confessing what God has done in you and facing the challenges you would otherwise have run from. Remember the Bible says: "the righteous are as bold as a lion" (Pr 28:1). You are the righteous of the Lord, so let the boldness that is in you flow out.

Chapter 12

Emotional and Psychological Healing

"You will surely forget your trouble, recalling it only as waters gone by"

Why do many people suffer from emotional and mental wounds from which they seem to never receive any form of healing? The simple reason is that they have not surrendered to the Lord the situation and the people that caused the pain in the first place. I have seen people living with hurts that were caused them several years or even decades ago. The pain is still as fresh as though it happened yesterday. The only reason for this is lack of forgiveness in the heart of such people who consider themselves victims of the wickedness of others.

It is not a natural human virtue to forgive. Forgiveness comes from God. And for Him to work out His forgiveness through us so that it extents to others, we must come to the point where we lay down our case for revenge at the foot of the cross. It is forgiveness that brings healing. True and total forgiveness brings total and complete healing. You were not meant to live with any hurt for any considerable amount of time. The Lord wants to bring healing to every wound in your heart, no matter how deep and devastating the wounds may have been. But for this to happen, you have to let go those you have begrudged because of the hurts they caused you, whether it was intentional or unintentional. You must allow the forgiveness of God to flow through you and reach the people who may have hurt you.

> *It is not a natural human virtue to forgive. Forgiveness comes from God. And for Him to work out His forgiveness through us so that it extents to others, we must come to the point where we lay down our case for revenge at the foot of the cross.*

I have heard people say, "I can forgive but I will never forget". This also is deception because true forgiveness makes you forget. Let the word of God be true and everything you have heard, or experienced, contrary to that be a blatant lie! It is possible to forget your troubles. The Bible says, you will forget your troubles, recalling it only as waters gone by. When water passes, the only thing you can remember is that water had passed. It passes and never returns. When you surrender your hurts to the Lord, "you will surely forget your trouble". Look at the qualifying word "surely". It means with certainty, without any possibility of failure, in a sure or certain manner; infallibly; undoubtedly; assuredly. The secret to permanent healing is surrender, absolute surrender to the Lord, of all that others have done to you and all that you have done to others.

It is the gateway to fruitfulness

Every hurt, wound, and pain that the Lord allowed to come to your life was designed to bring forth some fruits. The Bible says, "In him we were also chosen, having been predestined according to the plan of him who works out everything in conformity with the purpose of his will" (Eph 1:11). God works out everything to conform to the purpose of His will for your life. No matter how horrendous it may have seemed, it is possible for God to make it conform to the fruitfulness He had planned for you. The only hindrance to that can be you, when you refuse to forgive and be healed.

We find a good example of this in the story of Joseph. His brothers attempted to kill him but later changed their minds and sold him to the Ishmaelites who took him down to Egypt and sold him as a slave to Potiphar. He went through very serious difficulties but God in His faithfulness raised him to the second in command in Egypt. When his sons were born, this is what is written: "Before the years of famine came, two sons were born to Joseph by Asenath daughter of Potiphera, priest of On. Joseph named his firstborn Manasseh and said, "It is because God has made me forget all my trouble and all my father's household." The second son he named Ephraim and said, "It is because God has made me fruitful in the land of my suffering" (Ge 41:50-52).

Joseph had to be healed from his wounds before God could make him prosper in the land of his troubles. He had to forget his troubles before he could become twice fruitful. Manasseh must be brought forth before Ephraim can be born. Many people are longing for the Ephraims, that is, the fruitfulness that follows the trouble which come to us, but are trying to bypass the bringing forth of Manasseh, that is receiving of total healing from the Lord through absolute surrender. Surrender brings the blessing of inner healing which brings the blessing of fruitfulness.

> *True and total forgiveness brings total and complete healing. You were not meant to live with any hurt for any considerable amount of time. The Lord wants to bring healing to every wound in your heart, no matter how deep and devastating the wounds may have been.*

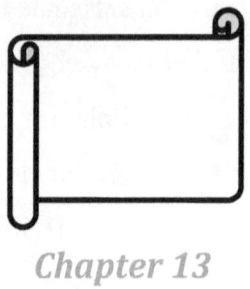

Chapter 13

Brightness of Life

"Life will be brighter than noonday, and darkness will become like morning."

It is written that, "The path of the righteous is like the morning sun, shining ever brighter till the full light of day" (Pr 4:18). The Lord has ordained that the paths we take in life be bright except in very few instances when He may want us to exercise faith by walking in the dark. His word is designed to be a lamp to our feet and a light unto our path. The degree of our surrender to the Lord in obedience to His word determines how bright our paths become. He wants us to take firm and secure steps as we walk the path to our destiny.

The light that comes from the word of God is brighter than the sun. However, it can be likened to the sun in that it begins with a low intensity of brightness which increases to its peak at noon. Though the sun's intensity begins to fall off after noon, the light that comes from the word never diminishes in intensity; it only keeps increasing as we walk in obedience to the word we have received. It shines ever brighter till the full light of day. The light we have today should be greater than the light we had yesterday. And the light we have tomorrow should be greater than the one we have today, if we stay on the path to destiny marked out for us by the Sovereign Lord. It takes a surrendered person to stay on the path of destiny established for him by God. And it takes a surrendered person to increasingly respond to the light of revelation received.

> The degree of our surrender to the Lord in obedience to His word determines how bright our paths become. He wants us to take firm and secure steps as we walk the path to our destiny.

It takes the Spirit and the word

There is a darkness that will increasingly cover the earth as we approach the end of this age. But the Lord has promised that for the child of God, though darkness covers the earth, light of His glory will shine. This promise is stated thus: "Arise, shine, for your light has come, and the glory of the LORD rises upon you. See, darkness covers the earth and thick darkness is over the peoples, but the LORD rises upon you and his glory appears over you. Nations will come to your light, and kings to the brightness of your dawn" (Is 60:1-3). What a promise for a bright life given us by the Lord.

The brightness of our lives does not depend on light from the surrounding. It comes from the glory of the King that appears to us in the midst of the deep darkness that surrounds the earth. Note what the Lord says, just before this promise is stated: "As for me, this is my covenant with them," says the LORD. "My Spirit, who is on you, will not depart from you, and my words that I have put in your mouth will always be on your lips, on the lips of your children and on the lips of their descendants—from this time on and forever," says the LORD" (Is 59:21). When you yield in covenant obedience to the leading of the Spirit and confess the word of God, you are placed where His glory rises upon you. When we surrender to the Spirit, and walk in the light of the word, we are sure to maintain and increase the brightness of the light around us. And this brightness sets you apart from the rest of the world and makes them run to you.

The beauty of the morning

Isaiah tells us that "Nations will come to your light, and kings to the brightness of your dawn". There is a mystery about the light of dawn that makes it desirable to nature. It's as if the whole of creation longs for the morning. This is especially known about humankind that it longs for the passing of the night and the dawning of the morning. This is because there is something about the night that brings terror, pain, and decay. When you have a pain, it seems to increase in the night. When food gets bad it does so overnight. Those who suffer from mental problems seem more agitated in the night. Patients on their sick beds long for the breaking of the dawn.

Conversely, those who dread the dawning light are thieves, witches and wizards, and those involved in shameful acts. It is in the night that pests like mosquitos and roaches come out to cause havoc. In a house infested with roaches, the turning off of the lights at night is the bell for their gathering and play. If by chance you get up in the night and turn on the light, you see them running for cover.

The morning however, unlike the night, brings with it new life and vitality, hope and expectations, and fills you with aspirations. The arrival of the morning light sends the pests into their hiding places. So if your night will become as the morning because of surrender, it means pests will have no place in your life. Surrender takes away the night and makes you dwell in perpetual morning light. Oh beloved, this has been experienced by saints throughout Christian history. And I believe with my whole heart that you and I can live in such a place. This is the Father's will for us, and the way to get there is through absolute surrender. "Darkness will become like morning". What a blessing! What a place to live in. There is a place in the Christian life called the Total Light Zone. In this place darkness has no access because the light ever shines. Let us all surrender to the Spirit, and walk in the light of the word, so that the glory may rise upon us and be a beacon to the nations and the kings of the earth.

> *The light we have today should be greater than the light we had yesterday. And the light we have tomorrow should be greater than the one we have today, if we stay on the path to destiny marked out for us by the Sovereign Lord*

Chapter 14

Security

"You will be secure, because there is hope…"

Hopelessness and lack of expectations are some factors of insecurity in the life of a person. When we come to the place of absolute surrender, the Lord breathes supernatural hope into our lives and fills us with expectation for what He has ordained for us to discover and fulfill. It is the Lord's will for us to live in absolute security, within and without. Security is one of God's promises to you; He says, '"I will strengthen them in the LORD and in his name they will live securely," declares the LORD' (Ze 10:12).

The Lord promises to strengthen you in Himself so that you can live securely in His name. Your security should not come from your country or family or spouse or job or relationships you have built, or whatever men may derive their security from. God wants your security to come from His name, and in His name.

It's such a fortress

Why many live insecure lives is because they are not sure of the protection they have. Remember I said that fear makes your life unstable and renders you ineffective, and that it is the fear of the Lord that drives out all other fears. He who truly fears God fears nothing else. And the Lord designed that the fear of Him will be a fortress for the believer. When you fear the Lord, you live in an impregnable fortress because the word says, "Whoever fears the LORD has a secure fortress, and for their children it will be a refuge" (Pr 14:26).

He says in the Bible, "Let the beloved of the LORD rest secure in him, for he shields him all day long, and the one the LORD loves rests between his shoulders" (Dt 38:12).

> *Your security should not come from your country or family or spouse or job or relationships you have built, or whatever men may derive their security from. God wants your security to come from His name, and in His name.*

Absolute surrender brings you to the place where you rest secure in Him. You are aware of the shield that the Lord provides for you every second of every day. There is a place of total security in the Lord, and surrender is the path you tread to reach there.

David lived in such a place

We have already made several references to David in this study of absolute surrender. We are going to make yet another reference to him. In my opinion, apart from the Lord of glory Himself, nobody else manifested a life of surrender as David. He fled from Saul and refused to start a rebellion against the Kingdom. He refused to kill Saul when he had the opportunity to do so more than once. He allowed his own son to chase him from the throne when he had the manpower to stop it before it happened. He allowed himself to be ridiculed and cursed by Shimei the Benjamite. He did all this because he believed his life was in the hands of his God. He knew the Lord had provided him the security he needed and had no cause for self-defense. In the midst of danger he wrote this Psalm which is a symbol of one who feels secure:

'LORD, how many are my foes! How many rise up against me! Many are saying of me, "God will not deliver him." But you, LORD, are a shield around me, my glory, the One who lifts my head high. I call out to the LORD, and he answers me from his holy mountain. I lie down and sleep; I wake again, because the LORD sustains me. I will not fear though tens of thousands assail me on every side. Arise, LORD! Deliver me, my God! Strike all my enemies on the jaw; break the teeth of the wicked. From the LORD comes deliverance. May your blessing be on your people"' (Ps 3).

When you surrender, you come to know the Lord as your shield, your glory, the One who lifts your head high, and your deliverer. Like David you can lay you down and sleep in the midst of the galloping of enemy horses and the marching boots of enemy combatants. And like him you will come to say, "It is God who arms me with strength and keeps my way secure" (2 Sa 22:33).

> *It is the Lord's will for us to live in absolute security, within and without. Security is one of God's promises to you.*

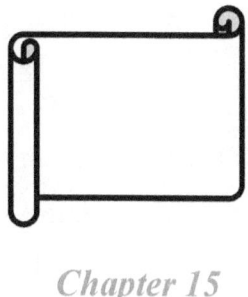

Chapter 15

Rest

"You will look about you and take your rest in safety. You will lie down, with no one to make you afraid"

When it comes to rest, there is both a promise and an invitation to God's rest. The Father wants us to enter into His rest not while we pass on to glory but while we still walk the face of this earth.

The promise

The Bible says, "There remains, then, a Sabbath-rest for the people of God; for anyone who enters God's rest also rests from their works, just as God did from his. Let us, therefore, make every effort to enter that rest, so that no one will perish by following their example of disobedience" (He 4:9-11).

There is a promised rest for each one of us, the rest of God. This is what the Bible calls a Sabbath-rest for the people of God. And just like any other promise of God, we have to make some effort to appropriate it and make it ours. And the Lord exhorts us to make every effort to enter that rest. In other words you should be willing to do whatever it takes for you to enter God's rest.

Recently the Lord has been working in me and bringing me to the place of absolute rest in Him. I was getting disturbed about a number of issues in my life and ministry which were not going as they ought to until I came to the point of surrendering even my success and all to the Lord. When we lay all at the altar of the Lord, and carry His own burden, we enter absolute rest.

The invitation

The Lord Jesus Christ said to us all, "Come to me, all you who are weary and burdened, and I will give you rest. Take my yoke upon you and learn from me, for I am gentle and humble in heart, and you will find rest for your souls. For my yoke is easy and my burden is light" (Mt 11:28-30). We enter rest by coming to the place of divine exchange; you give Him your weariness and your burdens for His easy yoke and light burden. Until we reach this point where we totally surrender all our worries, burdens and anxieties and take up the yoke (which is the commitment to do His will and delight in that which is in the heart of God) of the Lord upon our necks, we are not able to enter rest. There is rest for you, but there is a price to pay for it. And the price is your burdens and weariness, and the readiness to take His yoke upon you. He will not force His yoke upon your neck; it's up to you to willingly take it so that you can plow in the field of the Master.

The path to rest

This is what the LORD says: "Stand at the crossroads and look; ask for the ancient paths, ask where the good way is, and walk in it, and you will find rest for your souls" (Jer 6:16). There is a promise of rest, there is an invitation to rest, and there is a pathway to that rest. If you have believed the promise and want to respond to the invitation, then you must know the path that leads to the blessedness of God's rest. We already established the fact that surrendering is a requisite for God's rest. Now I want to establish the fact that surrendering is something that is continuous.

> *Rest is what gives you access to experiencing the power of God in every area of your life. God will not manifest His power in any area of your life in which you have not entered His rest. It is rest that gives God the mandate to manifest His power and might on your behalf. This is the deal; when you enter God's rest, He enters your labors.*

Each time we come to the crossroads of life, the Lord commands us to stand and look. That is, we are to stop and observe which path is in line with God's ancient laws, principles, statutes, and ordinances. We are then to ask the Holy Spirit which is the good way amongst the paths that are in agreement with the word of God. The way He approves of as the good way becomes our choice. Choosing what He has chosen leads us into the rest of God for our souls, that is, the mind, the will, and the emotions.

When you have entered rest

When you enter God's rest, does it mean you will never find yourself in a situation which seeks to make you agitated, worried, or anxious? On the contrary many things will now attempt to get your soul out of its position of rest. When this happens, the secret is to command your soul to find rest in the Lord. This is what kept the psalmist in continual rest in the Lord. He commanded his soul to find rest in God. May we maintain our rest by commanding our whole been to stay in God's rest, when everything is demanding us to do otherwise: "Yes, my soul, find rest in God; my hope comes from him" (Ps 62:5).

God's rest frees you from the struggle to make things happen on your own. You cease to try to please men and focus on the only thing that matters; pleasing God. Rest is what gives you access to experiencing the power of God in every area of your life. God will not manifest His power in any area of your life in which you have not entered His rest. It is rest that gives God the mandate to manifest His power and might on your behalf. This is the deal; when you enter God's rest, He enters your labors.

Chapter 16

People will seek your favor

"…and many will court your favor"

Earlier on, we saw that when we surrender completely to the Lord, He makes our life bright and causes nations and kings to come to the light of our dawn. Secondly, when we surrender to the Lord, He gives us favor instead of rejection and people start striving to identify with you. This is a direct effect of the glory of the Lord that rises upon you as a result of absolute surrender. We have seen people attracted to the sweet smelling aroma of the anointing. This however, is child's play compared to the attraction that the glory brings.

Moreover, as we will see, surrendering puts you in a position of authority and influence. This position of influence becomes evident to people and makes them court your favor. This is because when we are surrendered, the aroma of the glory of God from us to those around us. This aroma of God's glory will attract people to the ministry that God is doing through us.

Of Asher, it is written, "Most blessed of sons is Asher; let him be favored by his brothers, and let him bathe his feet in oil" (Dt 33:24). What a blessing! What a position to be in, where everyone shows you favor!

Friends in High Places

When people know that you have friends in high places, they will want to associate with you because you become a gate way to high places. The Bible talks of the days when "… ten people from all languages and nations will take firm hold of one Jew by the hem of his robe and say, 'Let us go with you, because we have heard that God is with you'" (Zec 8:23). Beloved this is the time for those of us who are in the Church of the Firstborn. But until we surrender to His will so that His glory and favor are evident upon us, we will not experience it.

Are you not tired of men hiding from you when they see you with your Bible? Are you not tired of being turned down when they realize you are born again? We are in the days of His favor upon His Church. It is time for the nations to court our favor. It is time for them to run to us with their needs and troubles. It is time for them to seek us for solutions that come from above. But we must come to the place of absolute surrender to the will of He who rules over all. We must surrender our own wisdom so that He fills us with divine wisdom. When His glory rises upon you, those who hid from you will come running after you. Those who mocked will celebrate you.

Job is an example of a man before whom people sought to find favor. He said of those days, "People listened to me expectantly, waiting in silence for my counsel. After I had spoken, they spoke no more; my words fell gently on their ears. They waited for me as for showers and drank in my words as the spring rain. When I smiled at them, they scarcely believed it; the light of my face was precious to them" (Job 29:21-24). As you surrender to the Lord may people long to hear you. May they listen to you with expectation! May they seek your counsel! May they long to see you smile at them! May the light of your face be precious to them! Amen!

> *We are in the days of His favor upon His Church. It is time for the nations to court our favor. It is time for them to run to us with their needs and troubles. It is time for them to seek us for solutions that come from above.*

Chapter 17

Riches in God

"… then the Almighty will be your gold, the choicest silver for you"

The Lord wants us to come to the point where He alone is our riches. Just as people value the least quantity of gold, we need to value the Lord. The power of surrender brings us to the realization that the only true riches we can ever have is God Himself. Surrender brings us to embrace God as the riches that are enough for time and for eternity.

Not God plus intellectual riches!

Not God plus material riches!

Not God plus social riches!

Not God plus financial riches!

Not God plus spiritual riches!

But God alone all sufficient, more than enough, is the riches we must pursue.

In the old Covenant, the priests were required to own nothing but have the Lord as their only possession. It was said of them,

"You will have no inheritance in their land, nor will you have any share among them; I am your share and your inheritance among the Israelites" (Dt 18:20).

"'I am to be the only inheritance the priests have. You are to give them no possession in Israel; I will be their possession" (Ez 44:28).

> *When all we have is God, then all He has and is becomes available to us. When the Almighty, El-Shaddai, the One who is all sufficient becomes all you have, then you are truly rich because you have unlimited access to the riches we have in Christ Jesus.*

This was an established statute for the descendants of Aaron and the rest of the Levitical family. The Lord was to be their only possession. In giving up everything to possess the Lord only, they turned out to receive the best of all that the other tribes owned. And because we are priests of the New Covenant, the Lord wants to bring us to the point where the gold and silver of this world mean nothing in comparison to having Him. But this must be done by our own will through absolute surrender.

There are times when nothing else matters to me but to just have Him and love Him. The sad thing is that I have failed to make that place my dwelling; that place where Jehovah is enough, where Jesus alone is my joy, strength, satisfaction, and motivation in life. The true riches of life is to have God, as one's only possession. And in having Him only, we possess everything. That is why Paul could paradoxically say, "...having nothing, and yet possessing everything..." (2Co 6:13).

The Lord wants to take us through the gateway of surrendering to the place where nothing else matters but to have Him in His fullness. In the eyes of men you may seem to be having nothing while you truly possess everything because the One who owns everything in this world is yours. Lord, help me return to that place where You alone are all that matters, where having You in Your fullness is the only one satisfaction my soul longs for. When we have nothing else but the Lord, like Peter and John we would be able to give the world nothing but Jesus. Like them we would say with confidence and sincerity, "silver or gold I do not have. But such as I have, in the name of Jesus…"

When all we have is God, then all He has and is becomes available to us. When the Almighty, El-Shaddai, the One who is all sufficient becomes all you have, then you are truly rich because you have unlimited access to the riches we have in Christ Jesus. May you experience absolute surrender so you can know him as the God who is more than enough!

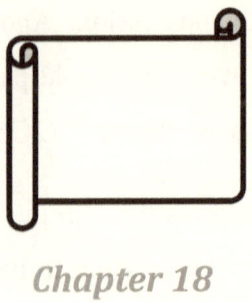

Chapter 18

Delight in the Almighty

"Surely then you will find delight in the Almighty and will lift up your face to God"

Another blessing that flows from a life that is surrendered to the Lord is the privilege to delight in the Lord and in Him only. It is a great blessing to find our pleasure and satisfaction in the Lord only. He is the only One who never changes or disappoints. So when you find your delight in the Lord Almighty, then your pleasure and satisfaction will be continuous. Absolute surrender is what brings you to the place of absolute delight in the God of the universe.

When you delight in something, you want to look at it, feel it, be around it, touch it, and admire it all day long. Because David's delight was in the Lord he could say, "One thing I ask from the LORD, this only do I seek: that I may dwell in the house of the LORD all the days of my life, to gaze on the beauty of the LORD and to seek him in his temple" (Ps 27:4). Delighting in the Lord will make you want to spend your time in His presence. It pushes you to the place of sweet fellowship and communion with the Lord.

As we delight in Him we fix our gaze on the beauty of His holiness and majesty. And the continuous gazing on the Lord transforms us into His likeness. This delight in the Lord makes you want to know Him more, love Him more, and serve Him more. Delight in the Lord makes everything else to fade and disappear in His sight. I have tasted of it. I know what it means to gaze on Him, as the beauty and sweetness of His presence permeates every fiber of my being. At such moments all I want is to stay in His presence and be with Him.

The gateway to fulfillment

The Bible commands us to, "Delight yourself in the LORD; And He will give you the desires of your heart" (Ps 37:4, NASB). And we saw that delight in the Lord is an offspring of surrender. Until we reach the place of absolute surrender, we can't truly delight in the Lord. When we delight in the Lord, He grants us the desires of our heart. What we want or desire is what He wants or desires for us. In this way our every desire will be met; and we will therefore live contented and fulfilled lives. Remember that, "Hope deferred makes the heart sick, but desire fulfilled is a tree of life" (Pr 13:12).

When we desire things that we can't get, it makes the heart sick and there is lack of fulfillment. But if we delight in the Lord, He grants our every desire, and the fulfilled desires lead to a fulfilled Christian life. This is the simple pathway to fulfillment and contentment. When we delight in Him, He makes our steps firm. That is, every step we take in life will have a firm hold and we will not be afraid of slipping and falling away. The fear of slipping and falling drains fulfillment in the Christian life. The psalmist said, "The LORD makes firm the steps of the one who delights in him; though he may stumble, he will not fall, for the LORD upholds him with his hand" (Ps 37:23-24).

Do you want your steps to be firm? Do you want to be upheld? Do you want to be kept from falling? Then the secret is to delight in the Lord by coming to the place of absolute surrender.

What it means Delighting in the Lord is not just something mental or emotional. It can actually be measured through its different manifestations. Delight in the Lord consists of the following aspects:

> *As we delight in Him, we fix our gaze on the beauty of His holiness and majesty. And the continuous gazing on the Lord transforms us into His likeness.*

- *Delight in His word*: the first evidence of delight in the Lord is delight in His word. The word of God is His primary voice on the earth. And just as we enjoy listening to someone we delight in, so when we delight in the Lord we enjoy listening to His voice by reading, studying, and meditating on His word continuously. That is why the psalmist said, "Blessed is the man that walketh not in the counsel of the ungodly, nor standeth in the way of sinners, nor sitteth in the seat of the scornful. But his delight is in the law of the LORD; and in his law doth he meditate day and night. And he shall be like a tree planted by the rivers of water, that bringeth forth his fruit in his season; his leaf also shall not wither; and whatsoever he doeth shall prosper" (Ps 1:1-3, KJV).

- *Delight in His works*: the second evidence of delighting in the Lord is to delight in His works. The works of the Lord include creation, salvation, healing, and deliverance. When we delight in His works we do everything to promote the works of the Lord in the lives of others, and to protect what He has accomplished in us. Here are some verses that talk of what we are saying:

    "Great are the works of the LORD; they are pondered by all who delight in them" (Ps 111:2).

    "Then my soul will rejoice in the LORD and delight in his salvation" (Ps 35:9).

- *Delight in His will*: the third evidence of delight in the Lord is delight in His will. When we delight in Him, His will becomes like the very breath we take and nothing else brings pleasure or satisfaction but doing the will of God. The psalmist, prophetically talking of the Messiah said, "Sacrifice and offering thou didst not desire; mine ears hast thou opened: burnt offering and sin offering hast thou not required. Then said I, Lo, I come: in the volume of the book it is written of me, I delight to do thy will, O my God: yea, thy law is within my heart" (Ps 40:6-8, KJV). When we delight in Him, we don't do things because they are considered a sacrifice or an offering to the Lord, we do things because we are convinced they are His will, as written in the Book. We want to find out what that will is at each stage of our life.

- *Delight in His worship*: the fourth evidence of delight in the Lord is that we desire to come to His altar in praise and worship. We delight to pour out our heart before our God in passionate worship and praise. We create opportunities in the course of our day to worship Him in our thoughts, words and actions: "Then I will go to the altar of God, to God, my joy and my delight. I will praise you with the lyre, O God, my God" (Ps 43:4).

Chapter 19

Guaranteed Answer to Prayer

"You will pray to him, and he will hear you, and you will fulfill your vows"

Are you not tired of unanswered prayers? Are you not tired of being in a position where answers to prayers are a 50-50 game? This is not how it was meant to be. The Lord so designed that every prayer we make should be answered. The problem with our prayers is that we often pray out of selfish or ambitious motives and reasons. That is why James said, "When you ask, you do not receive, because you ask with wrong motives, that you may spend what you get on your pleasures" (Jas 4:3).

Surrender brings you to the place where you want to spend everything on His pleasures and the things which bring Him delight and laughter. In the last section we just looked at what it is to delight in the Lord, which is one of the blessings of a life that is surrendered to the Lord. Now when we delight in Him, we automatically delight in His word, His works, His will, and worship. At this point, every prayer we make will be in accordance with His word, His works, His will, and His worship. Is there anyway such a prayer can go unanswered?

When the apostle John wrote, "This is the confidence we have in approaching God: that if we ask anything according to his will, he hears us. And if we know that he hears us—whatever we ask—we know that we have what we asked of him" (1Jn 5:14-15), he was writing with the intent that we all will live permanently in a place of absolute surrender to the Lord.

Think of it! Your every request is met, your every prayer is answered. All what it takes, and I must admit it's a difficult place to reach, is to ask nothing until we are sure that it's in accord with His word, His works, and His will. That is the place the Son of God lived in throughout His life on this planet earth. Remember He said to the Father, "Father, I thank you that you have heard me. I knew that you always hear me…" (Jn 11:41). Now, this is confidence! And this is the kind of confidence the Father wants us to have when we come to Him in prayer. But He will only put such confidence in us when we reach the place of absolute surrender. Then His grace and power can flow through us unhindered, to touch the lives and situations that we bring before Him in prayer and supplication.

I want to let you know faith is not something that originates from man. It is imparted to us by the Holy Spirit through the word, and as we desire to fulfill the will of the Father. This is the place I want to be. I desire, and am determined to exert every effort and pay any price to reach this place and to abide there, a place where even one's wishes are transmitted to the throne of grace by the Holy Spirit. That place where the Father Himself said, "Before they call I will answer; while they are still speaking I will hear" (Is 65:24).

Chapter 20

Heaven's backing on your Decisions

"Thou shalt also decree a thing, and it shall be established unto thee: and the light shall shine upon thy ways" (v 28, KJV).

Surrender brings us to a place of influence and authority in the courts of the King of heaven. When we have influence in the courts of the Ruler of the universe, it means all creation is bound to listen to us when we speak of things visible and invisible. Authority in the courts of heaven means authority in every other realm below. The Bible says we are seated with Christ in heavenly places. And Christ is seated at the right hand of God the Father. The right hand symbolizes authority.

The question is, why do many of us live lives that portray us to be at the mercy of the things that be? Heavenly authority can only be exercised on earth by men and women who are in position of absolute surrender, men and women who would not use that authority for self-promotion, self-defense, and self-gain. It is surrender that provides the gradient for a flow of the authority from the throne and through us.

Power to decree

It is one thing to decree a thing, and a totally different thing to decree a thing and have the backing of heaven on your decree. Are you not tired of making decrees that never come into effect? Oh, I have tasted the sweetness of passing decrees and seeing them fulfilled because heaven backed them. It is heaven's backing that gives our decrees angelic enforcement. It is heaven's backing that makes nature recognize the words we speak and obey. It is heaven's backing that makes principalities and powers in obey the words that we speak.

> Surrender brings us to a place of influence and authority in the courts of the King of heaven. When we have influence in the courts of the Ruler of the universe, it means all creation is bound to listen to us when we speak of things visible and invisible.

The Father wants us to exercise His authority on this earth without any apology. Remember the Lord Jesus Christ said, " Truly I tell you, if you have faith as small as a mustard seed, you can say to this mountain, 'Move from here to there,' and it will move. Nothing will be impossible for you"(Mt 17:20) and, "Truly I tell you, if you have faith and do not doubt, not only can you do what was done to the fig tree, but also you can say to this mountain, 'Go, throw yourself into the sea,' and it will be done"

(Mt 21:21). That is the kind of power to decree that the Lord wants us to have in this earth realm. But the truth is that very few people are there yet.

Let this blow your mind

This is what the Lord has said about Himself with respect to His servants and messengers, "…who carries out the words of his servants and fulfills the predictions of his messengers, who says of Jerusalem, 'It shall be inhabited,' of the towns of Judah, 'They shall be rebuilt,' and of their ruins, 'I will restore them'" (Is 44:26).

The Lord wants us to make decrees in sync with what He is doing in the realm of the Spirit. When we make such decrees, He carries then out for us. What a place of honor and privilege. How wonderful, how great, how awesome is our God. He wants to carry out your words and fulfill your decrees. Remember what Elijah told Ahab: "As the LORD, the God of Israel, lives, whom I serve, there will be neither dew nor rain in the next few years except at my word." Wow! Elijah said except at his word. His word brought the drought. And his word ended the drought. Notice that Elijah did not say the word of the Lord. He said, his word, that is, the word of Elijah. Now this is authority with God and with men. It is his word that brought fire from heaven to consume two groups of soldiers who came to arrest him. Oh! For the grace to absolutely surrender so as to reach such a place of total authority!

Chapter 21

Fulfilling your priestly role of intercession

"When people are brought low and you say, 'Lift them up!' then he will save the downcast. He will deliver even one who is not innocent, who will be delivered through the cleanness of your hands."

One of the privileged roles we have as priests of the New Covenant is that of intercessors. The simple truth is that many of us have not come to the point of absolute surrender of our time, our will, our priorities, and our personal biases. These must all be laid at the foot of the cross if we must fulfill the role of intercession. Absolute surrender brings you to a neutral position in every matter so you can discern the will of God and intercede in line with it. It is so vital for us to be in such a place so that the intercessions we make are free from personal biases and inclinations. As such we will be willing to devote the time required to receive answers, and give intercession the priority it deserves in our walk with the Lord.

Surrender is essential for us to fulfill this role because the Lord may need you to intercede for situations which are contrary to your mindset, likes, or natural inclinations. He may call you to intercede for a people, tribe, or nation you do not like. He may call you to intercede for a cause or ministry you consider rival. This is why surrender is absolutely necessary to fulfill the role of intercessor. Moses fulfilled this role even for a people who rejected his leadership and opposed him in every turn. He stood in the gap and prevented their elimination from the face of the earth. Aaron equally interceded for those who wanted his overthrow from the priesthood.

The promise above says when we are in the place of absolute surrender, God is able to raise people, who have been brought low for whatever reason, if we ask Him to save them and lift them up. Even if the person(s) is guilty, the verse lets us know that God will deliver him because of our intercession. For you to be the intercessor God ordained you to be you will have to go through the gates of absolute surrender. And may the Lord help you to reach there.

> Absolute surrender brings you to a neutral position in every matter so you can discern the will of God and intercede in line with it. It is so vital for us to be in such a place so that the intercessions we make are free from personal biases and inclinations.

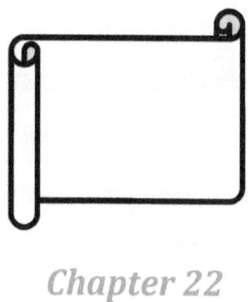

Chapter 22

Fruitfulness

'Simon answered, "Master, we've worked hard all night and haven't caught anything. But because you say so, I will let down the nets." When they had done so, they caught such a large number of fish that their nets began to break. So they signaled their partners in the other boat to come and help them, and they came and filled both boats so full that they began to sink' (Lk 5:5-7).

Another blessing of surrendering is the bearing of abundant fruits. The Lord said the Father's glory is for us to bear much fruit. This applies to the fruit of the Spirit, the fruit of repentance, and the fruit of discipleship. Many times we toil needlessly, doing what we know how to do yet we turn out without any fruits. So many people in this race are discouraged because of fruitlessness. Some have even given up any attempt to bring forth fruit because of repeated failure.

Like Peter in the passage above, many are washing their nets in total discouragement, disillusionment, disappointment and dismay. The first thing I want you to note here is that Peter first surrendered his boat for the Master's use. He was willing to stay there apparently doing nothing, and wasting his time while the Master used his boat to reach out to others. I am quite sure Peter needed to rest after a toilsome night with nothing to show for it. But he surrendered the right to his time and rest so the Master could use it for the Kingdom.

The second thing is that he obeyed the Master to launch into the deep even when this was contrary to what he knew his whole life as a professional fisherman. This is what surrendering does; it brings you the point where you are willing and ready to follow instructions given by the Spirit even when contrary to visible evidences, experiences, and the counsel of carnal men.

Because He says so

For us to bear the fruit we are destined to in every area of our lives, be it spiritual, social, financial, material, or professional, we need to come to the point where our actions are carried out "because He says so". It is the same as saying "not my will but yours be done" or "may it be to me according to your word". These are all statements of absolute surrender. And those who have said it from sincere hearts have always been blessed beyond their greatest imaginations.

Just as the branch of a tree depends on the vine, and is surrendered to the vine, so we ought to be surrendered to Him for us to bear the fruit we ought to bear. When Peter obeyed because He said so, we are told that he caught such a large number of fish that his boat alone could not contain, so he had to beckon on his fellow fishermen to come to his rescue and share the blessings of abundant fruitfulness. The gateway to fruit bearing is absolute surrender!

> For us to bear the fruit we are destined to in every area of our lives, be it spiritual, social, financial, material, or professional, we need to come to the point where our actions are carried out "because He says so".

Conclusion

The place of absolute surrender to the Lord is the place where we come to enter into the fullness of our inheritance in Him. It is the place of fulfillment, power and authority, abundant life. It is the place where Christ is fully expressed through our daily choices. Because of the great rewards when you dwell in such a place, the enemy will do his best to prevent you from getting there and keep you from dwelling there if you ever make it. However, as you yield to the leading of the Master, He will hold your hand each step of the way and take you there. Do not settle for anything less!

If you have been blessed by the message we have shared in this book, do not hesitate to share your testimony with us.

www.ingramcontent.com/pod-product-compliance
Lightning Source LLC
Chambersburg PA
CBHW021155080526
44588CB00008B/347